POLAR ANIMALS

Explore the Fascinating Worlds of . . .

CARIBOU
by Julia Vogel

PENGUINS
by Cherie Winner

POLAR BEARS
by Linda Tagliaferro

SEALS
by Wayne Lynch

Illustrations by John F. McGee

NorthWord Press
Chanhassen, Minnesota

Photography © 2002: Jim Brandenburg/Minden Pictures: p. 13; Craig Brandt: pp.4, 6, 21, 27, 43, 46; Robin Brandt: p. 59; Brandon D. Cole: p. 160; Tui De Roy/Minden Pictures: pp. 53, 61, 65, 66-67, 157; David B. Fleetham/Tom Stack & Associates: p. 144; Florian Graner/Seapics.com: pp. 162-163; Michio Hoshino/Minden Pictures: pp. 22, 31, 101, 112-113, 118, 137, 179; Lisa & Mike Husar/Team Husar: pp. 96, 108-109, 122, 130-131, 136; Don Jones: p. 42; Steven Kazlowski/Seapics.com: cover, pp. 104, 115, 133; Frans Lanting/Minden Pictures: pp. 78, 82; Tom & Pat Leeson: p. 56; Wayne Lynch: pp. 14-15, 50, 52, 54-55, 58, 70, 73, 74, 77, 81, 88-89, 92, 98, 99, 123, 124, 126-127, 134-135, 142, 145, 146-147, 149, 150, 152-153, 154, 158-149, 165, 166-167, 168, 169, 170, 172-173, 174, 176-177, 180, 181, 184; Amos Nachoum/Seapics.com: pp. 102-103, 138; Flip Nicklin/Minden Pictures: pp. 116-117; Mark Raycroft: pp. 18, 40-41; Claude Steelman/www.wildshots.com: p. 129; Gene & Jason Stone/Leeson Photography pp. 44-45; Mark J. Thomas/Dembinsky Photo Assoc.: p. 120-121; Vic Van Ballenberghe: p. 16; Tom Vezo: pp. 7, 28-29; Ingrid Visser/Seapics.com: p. 114; Tom Walker: pp. 8, 19, 24-25, 34-35, 36, 37, 62; Glenn Williams/Minden Pictures: p. 110; Art Wolfe: pp. 10-11, 68, 84-85, 87, 90-91, 106.

NorthWord Press
18705 Lake Drive East
Chanhassen, MN 55317
1-800-328-3895
www.northwordpress.com

Illustrations by John F. McGee

Library of Congress Cataloging-in-Publication Data
Polar animals : explore the fascinating words of-- / by Julia Vogel ... [et al.];
illustrations by John F. McGee.
   p. cm.
  Contents: Caribou / by Julia Vogel -- Penguins by Cherie Winner -- Polar bears / by
Linda Tagliaferro -- Seals / by Wayne Lynch.
  ISBN 1-55971-832-3 (hard cover)
  1. Zoology--Polar regions--Juvenile literature. [1. Zoology-- Polar regions. 2. Caribou.
3. Penguins. 4. Polar bear. 5. Bears. 6. Seals (Animals)] I. Vogel, Julia. II. McGee, John
F., ill.

QL104 .P63 2002
590'.911--dc21   2002019003

Printed in Singapore   10 9 8 7 6 5 4 3 2 1

POLAR ANIMALS

TABLE OF CONTENTS

Explore the Fascinating World of . . .

Caribou

Julia Vogel
Illustrations by John F. McGee

CARIBOU ARE ALWAYS on the move. Every spring, large groups, or herds, march north to spend the summer near the Arctic Ocean. Every fall, they journey south again for the winter. World-champion walkers, caribou have followed the same trails through northern wilderness for thousands of years. This seasonal movement is called migration. For caribou, migration may be hundreds of miles long!

These ancient wanderers make their home in one of the harshest places on Earth. They must withstand the Arctic's strong winds, deep snow, and frigid temperatures. How do caribou survive in this frozen land?

Caribou antlers come in all sizes and shapes. This male's unique antlers can be used to easily identify him.

A young caribou is called a calf. It stays near its mother for protection and for food.

Like caribou this reindeer has excellent senses. It can hear and see especially well. And its sense of smell is much better than a human's.

Caribou belong to a group of large mammals, the deer family. Moose, whitetail deer, and elk are also members of this family. All kinds of deer share important features, or traits, that help them survive. Long necks help them see far to spot danger, and slim legs provide power for quick escapes. Hooves, or hard coverings on their feet, grip the ground wherever they walk. And members of the deer family are the only animals that grow bony antlers on their heads, which they use to fight off predators (PRED-uh-torz), or animals that kill them for food.

Moose and elk also live in cold climates, but caribou live farther north than any of their close relatives. Caribou are stockier and have shorter legs than many other family members. These are two traits that help them stay warm.

During the last Ice Age, millions of caribou roamed North America's snow fields with mammoths, mastodons, and other creatures that have become extinct, or died out. Caribou fossils have been found as far south as Tennessee and Alabama. The areas where caribou live and feed are called home ranges. As the Earth warmed, the herds' living space became smaller. Today, nearly all of North America's caribou live in Alaska and Canada.

Caribou
FUNFACT:

Caribou and reindeer belong to the same species, and have the same scientific name, *Rangifer tarandus*. There are about 3 million wild caribou in the world, plus about 2 million wild and domesticated reindeer.

Unlike caribou, reindeer males are often known as stags and females are called does.

In Europe and Asia, caribou are known by another name, reindeer. Wild reindeer look and act very much like North American caribou, although reindeer are usually a bit smaller than caribou.

Many reindeer were domesticated, or tamed, about 5,000 years ago by native people in Asia's Altai Mountains. The tribes began following the herds, defending them from wolves, and using them for milk, meat, and hides. Some reindeer have been trained to pull sleds and carry riders. A century ago, tame reindeer were brought to Alaska to be herded by Eskimos. Today, natives in Scandinavia and Russia keep large reindeer herds to make a living in their icy homelands.

Woodland Caribou

Peary Caribou

Barren-ground Caribou

Peary caribou usually live in small herds. During summer, they feast on willow, herbs, and grasses. During winter, they search for whatever is available.

North America's caribou are separated into three main types. The smallest ones, Peary caribou, live the closest to the North Pole. Their home is on a few windswept islands in Canada's High Arctic. Every winter, they face extreme cold and darkness when the sun disappears from view for many weeks.

Their silky, white coat acts as camouflage (KAM-uh-flaj) to help them blend into their snow-white habitat, or surroundings. When spring returns, Peary caribou travel to find more food and safe places to give birth on the northern parts of their islands. They may even cross frozen ice to reach other shores. Recent bad weather has made their lives harder than ever, and only about 2,000 to 3,000 Peary caribou still exist on their rocky island homes.

Woodland caribou are found farther south than Peary caribou. These caribou live in the taiga (tie-GUH), a wide area of evergreen forests that is snow-covered in winter and boggy in summer. In North America, woodland caribou once roamed the northern United States from Maine to Washington. Hunting and clearing forests for farms have caused their populations to shrink and even vanish in some areas. Now almost all woodland caribou live in Canada's taiga, from Newfoundland to British Columbia.

Woodland caribou are the largest type, with extra-long legs for plowing through deep forest snow. Woodland caribou usually do not migrate long distances between summer and winter homes. But they are constantly going somewhere, searching for food or safe places to give birth or escaping from wolves, bears, and other predators.

Scientists are not sure why caribou have a patch of long hair, called a mane, around their necks. It may help the males look bigger and stronger to the females.

Caribou are diurnal (di-YER-nul) animals. That means they are mostly active during the day, when they move around and feed.

Wandering in small, scattered groups of two to six animals, woodland caribou avoid roads, houses, and even scientists trying to study them. Logging and road-building can chase them out of a forest and keep them away for decades. The woodland caribou's secretive ways have earned them the nickname, "gray ghosts of the forest."

In the winter, the taiga's trees also shelter another type of caribou, barren-ground caribou. But every spring, these caribou migrate north to the wide-open, treeless tundra (TUN-druh). Trees cannot grow on the tundra because of its extreme cold, strong winds, and ground that never thaws completely. The summer sun can melt only the top layer of earth, creating a marshy plain, green with grasses and other small plants. Canadians call the tundra "the barrens" because it looks like a frozen desert in winter, and that's probably where barren-ground caribou got their name. But in summer, the tundra is home to many creatures, including great numbers of birds and insects.

Caribou
FUNFACT:

Three herds have more than 500,000 animals: Western Arctic caribou herd of Alaska, George River caribou herd of Canada, and Taimyr Peninsula reindeer herd of Russia. The only wild caribou in the lower 48 states are about three dozen that live part of the year in the Selkirk Mountains of Idaho and Washington.

A male's antlers are often known as his rack.
The tips of the antlers are called points.

Living from Alaska to the Hudson Bay, barren-ground caribou are by far the most common type of caribou. They live in herds of a few thousand to over 500,000 animals. They are usually lighter-colored and smaller than woodland caribou, although sizes vary widely depending on where the animals live.

Adults stand about 3 to 5 feet (0.9 to 1.5 meters) tall at the shoulder. Females, or cows, weigh between 130 and 210 pounds (60 and 95 kilograms). Males, or bulls, may weigh as much as 175 to 400 pounds (80 to 180 kilograms).

Barren-ground males carry the widest and longest antlers of any caribou. One record pair was 46 inches (117 centimeters) wide and 51 inches (130 centimeters) long.

When caribou like this barren-ground herd graze, they move quickly.

But the barren-ground caribou's most spectacular feature is their seasonal migration. Depending on the herd, they may travel up to 600 miles (965 kilometers) between their summer and winter ranges—the longest migration of any land animal.

Wherever barren-ground caribou travel, native people have come to depend on them. Some tribes learned to follow the herds, while others built their villages along traditional migration paths. For thousands of years, caribou hides have been made into boots, robes, leggings, and tents. Knives, scrapers, spear points, and sewing needles have been shaped from bones and antlers. Many northern communities still rely on barren-ground caribou meat to help them survive the Arctic winter.

Every caribou needs a thick fur coat for protection from wind and cold. Hair covers them from their ears to their feet. In fact, caribou and moose are the only deer family members with fur all over their muzzles, or snouts.

Two kinds of hair insulate caribou in winter. A fine, curly underfur lies close to the body, warming it like a wool sweater. Longer, stiff guard hairs stand out to shed snow and block the wind. The guard hairs are hollow, and air trapped inside them makes an extra shield against the cold. These air-filled hairs also work like a life jacket, helping caribou float when they swim across lakes and rivers.

In cold weather, lots of body heat could escape through a caribou's long legs. But a network of arteries and veins cools caribou blood before it enters the legs, then warms it again as it returns to the body. A caribou's normal body temperature is about 102 degrees Fahrenheit (39 degrees Celsius), yet its legs stay around 46 degrees Fahrenheit (8 degrees Celsius). This system keeps needed heat from escaping when the wind whips around the caribou's legs.

All mammals with hooves on their feet are called ungulates (UN-gyoo-lutz). Caribou are even-toed ungulates, as are cows, pigs, and other deer. Each caribou foot has four toes: two big toes, and two smaller toes, called dew claws. Ungulates with an odd number of toes include horses, which have one toe on each foot, and rhinoceroses, with three toes on each foot.

Caribou
FUNFACT:

Caribou click when they walk! The sound is caused by their ankle tendons slipping over bones in their feet. It doesn't hurt the animal, but a large herd trotting along the trail can be very loud.

Caribou usually have white hair around the rump and muzzle and a ring around the eyes. They also have white hair inside the ears and sometimes a white chest patch.

Caribou can find their way straight across a lake too wide to see the other side. They are good swimmers.

The edges of caribou hooves are sharp, perfect for gripping the ice or for slashing at an attacking enemy. In the water, the wide hooves act like paddles to help the animal swim. In soft snow or swampy ground, the big toes and dew claws spread out, working like snowshoes to stop the caribou from sinking. Including the dew claws, a large male's track may be almost 8 inches (20 centimeters) long and more than 5 inches (13 centimeters) wide.

Perhaps the most important job of caribou hooves is digging for food. During much of the year, almost everything caribou eat is blanketed by snow. A hungry caribou uses its hooves like scoops, making quick pawing strokes to send snow flying out of the way. It must dig snow holes, called craters, throughout the winter to avoid starvation. Micmac Indians even named the animals "xalibu" (GHAH-lee-boo), meaning snow shoveler. Many people believe the word caribou comes from that Micmac name.

How do caribou find the food that is covered by snow? They rely on their keen sense of smell. They push their long, wide snouts into the snow, searching for food smells before beginning the difficult work of digging. Just as we can smell brownies in the oven, a caribou can easily smell food under 1 foot (30 centimeters) of snow. Caribou also use their noses to recognize each other and to detect danger.

Caribou are plant-eaters, or herbivores (HERB-uh-vorz). During the short Arctic summer, their diet includes many kinds of plants. Depending on where it lives, a caribou may eat Arctic cottongrass, willow leaves, mushrooms, and especially flower buds, which are packed with protein. An adult consumes 12 to 20 pounds (5 to 9 kilograms) per day.

Feeding grounds are not always on flat land. And bulls do not always graze alone. A good supply of food may attract several caribou.

Winter food in the Arctic, though, is scarce. Some days, the only things to eat are a few twigs, plus some snow for moisture. Luckily, one kind of caribou food is plentiful under the snow: lichens (LIE-kenz). Lichens are found year-round in strange, colorful splotches on rocks, tree branches, and frozen soil. Caribou eat so much of one kind of lichen, it's known as "reindeer moss" or "caribou candy."

The animals' huge appetites make it hard for the lichens to survive. A herd digging into drifts and stretching into trees for food can eventually strip an area through feeding and trampling. Brittle and easily damaged by sharp hooves, lichens grow slowly, only about ¼ inch (6 millimeters) per year. It can take 50 to 100 years, or more, for a forest to recover from too much grazing. Fortunately, the animals' constant wandering helps protect the lichens.

Whether they're eating fresh grass shoots or frozen lichens, caribou nip and tear off bites using their tongue and their bottom front teeth. They don't have incisors (in-SIZE-orz), or middle teeth, in their upper jaws. Their back teeth, or molars, grind the food just enough for it to be swallowed.

The partially chewed food travels to the first chamber of the caribou's four-chamber stomach. The animal looks for a safe place to rest, such as a frozen lake where predators can't sneak up on it without being seen. Then it brings a wad of food back into its mouth for re-chewing. The wads are called cuds, and caribou, like cattle, are called cud chewers. Once the cud is thoroughly chewed, it returns to the stomach, by-passing the first chamber and moving through each of the other three chambers to complete its digestion.

Even when caribou lie down to rest while chewing their cuds, they are always aware of their surroundings and the predators that may be nearby.

If this male and female sense a danger to the herd, they call to the others.
If they run to escape, others then follow.

Even when eating or resting, caribou must stay alert to danger. Their sharp hearing helps keep them alive. The cup-shaped ears collect sounds from near and far. And by swiveling their ears, caribou can hear in almost any direction without turning their heads.

A caribou's eyes are large and can see close and far away. Positioned on the sides of the head, the eyes capture a wide field of view. Caribou don't see colors as we do. But they do see shapes clearly and can detect slight movements that a human would never notice.

At the first sign of danger, a caribou stops and sniffs the air. Then it signals the other herd members by snorting and kicking a hind leg out to the side. That's an alarm movement that all the others in a herd recognize. As the caribou leaps away, glands in its hind feet release a scent, or odor, that warns other caribou to beware of trouble. The startled caribou gallops away, then slows to a steady trot for many miles until it feels safe again.

Speed is a caribou's best defense against predators. But it may not always escape. A newborn may be grabbed in the forest by a lynx or snatched from above by a golden eagle. A mother caribou will try to defend her young by kicking or by slashing with her antlers. But she's usually no match for a grizzly bear that may be hunting to feed its own cubs.

One wild animal kills more caribou than any other: the wolf. Wolf packs follow caribou as they roam, watching and waiting. Because caribou run so fast, a single wolf rarely catches one. But a pack of wolves can work as a team. They sneak up on a caribou and ambush it, or separate a caribou from the herd, then chase it for miles to wear it down. The whole pack joins in the meal after a successful hunt.

To escape predators, caribou can run up to 50 miles per hour (80 kilometers per hour) on land. To get away, they are not afraid to run through a pond or river if necessary.

Leftovers from a wolf kill may be food for other hungry animals, such as wolverines, ravens, Arctic foxes, and even mice and voles. Biologists often call the caribou a keystone species because it is key, or important, to the survival of so many other Arctic animals.

Escaping from wolves is one reason barren-ground caribou migrate. Arctic wolves usually don't raise their young on the tundra, so most packs stay behind when the caribou herds leave the taiga in spring. Caribou also migrate to find the most nutritious food and to find the best places to live as the weather changes each season.

Longer days in springtime probably trigger the caribou's urge to travel. But how do they navigate, or find their way? Often, herds follow old trails they can clearly see on the land. But they must also climb snow-covered mountains, swim wide lakes, and wade across bogs or swamps. Have caribou memorized the routes? Are they following the wind, the stars, or Earth's magnetic clues? Researchers can now learn about caribou movements by following signals from special caribou collars, but they still haven't solved all the mysteries of caribou migration.

No matter how they navigate, we know caribou migration usually begins in April. Older, experienced cows lead the way, followed closely by other cows and last year's babies, or calves. Bulls age two and older often leave the taiga weeks later. The leading cows have the most difficult job, often needing to break through deep snow to make a good trail. The others follow single-file behind them to save energy for the long journey ahead.

Storms may slow their progress, or they may lose hours searching for a safe river crossing. Caribou in a hurry can travel up to 50 miles (80 kilometers) in a day. When they can walk no farther, the animals drop to the ground, exhausted. Yet hours later, they are up and ready to go on.

Each herd marches toward a different place on the tundra, where generations of their ancestors have been born. All caribou that share the same birthplace, or calving ground, belong to the same herd. For example, caribou born near the coast in the northeast corner of Alaska belong to the Porcupine herd. And those that return to Bluenose Lake in Canada are called the Bluenose herd.

While on the move, a caribou herd may travel in a line many miles long.
The animals often gather in groups to graze along the migration route.

At first, caribou calves are wobbly on their feet. They soon learn to keep up with their mother and the other calves in the herd.

By early June it is time for the calves to be born. Each cow separates from the herd to give birth alone. She searches for a quiet and protected place. A caribou has one calf per year, almost never twins. She licks her newborn clean, getting to know its unique smell and voice from all the other thousands of calves in her herd.

Nearly all the cows in the same herd give birth within about two weeks. This is called synchronous (SIN-kruh-nus) arrival. It helps protect the young from predators because there are too many calves to kill all at once. It also means the calves will have many playmates as they grow and learn about their habitat.

The newborns' color is reddish brown, which helps them blend into the brown tundra. But calves do not hide. They are following after their mothers within hours of their birth. In a few days the pair rejoins the herd. At seven days old, most calves can outrun a wolf.

The calves grow fast on their mother's milk, which is very rich. At birth, calves may weigh from 6 to 20 pounds (3 to 9 kilograms). Their weight doubles in about two weeks. They gain strength quickly too. Calves leap, twist, buck, chase each other, and run circles around their mothers. This is play that builds muscles and bones.

By late June, the strong summer sun turns the tundra green and calves begin nibbling on the tender plant growth. By mid-summer, most of them no longer need their mothers' milk. Caribou of all ages feast on their favorite plants. New mothers, especially, must eat as much as they can to recover from giving birth and to fatten-up for the long winter ahead.

Soon the mother takes the young caribou back to the herd, where they both will be safer.

In July, another kind of creature feasts on caribou: blood-sucking insects. Mosquitoes and biting flies hatch by the billions in the marshy tundra. At the same time, the caribou are shedding their heavy winter coat. This leaves only a thin layer of dark fur protecting their skin. The biting swarms torment and weaken the caribou. Mosquitoes can cause a caribou to lose up to 1 quart (0.95 liter) of blood each week during mosquito season.

Warm, windless days are the worst.

The fierce bites become more than the animals can stand. How they escape depends on where they live. Some climb slopes to reach cooling patches of snow. Others trot to the shore to stand in the breeze or wade into the waves. Often, groups of caribou gather together, standing tightly against one another so that each caribou has less chance of being bitten. These groups roam across the tundra, eating when they can, but moving fast to stay ahead of the insects.

The huge July gatherings make tremendous noise. The air seems filled with snorts, coughs, belches, and hoof beats. Calves bleat, or call, to their mothers, who grunt in reply. If a calf loses its mother, it stops. The mother stops too and lets the herd move on. Both trot back and forth along the trail, calling for each other, until they are reunited. But if they don't meet, the calf will probably die because another caribou cow will not adopt an orphan calf. Each cow only takes care of her own young.

True insect relief only comes with the cooler days of August. This is also the time that caribou scatter across the tundra for a final fattening-up before winter.

In early autumn, the animals begin to look different. Their new winter coats are chocolate brown, with a thick white mane on the neck and chest. Also during this time, bulls often add an extra layer of fat on the back and rump. It may be more than 3 inches (7.5 centimeters) thick. This fat will provide much needed energy during the upcoming breeding season, or rut.

But the biggest change to caribou appearance is on their heads. The adults' antlers are nearing full size, and even the calves have grown short spikes. Antlers average 20 to 51 inches (51 to 130 centimeters) long on adult males, and 9 to 20 inches (23 to 51 centimeters) long on adult females.

Caribou
FUNFACT:

Caribou recycle their own shed antlers by chewing on them to get calcium. Other creatures such as mice also nibble on the fallen antlers over the winter.

Broken branches give clues that a caribou has used a bush for antler polishing. Even a small animal can cause lots of damage.

The horns of cattle and some other animals grow all their lives. But antlers grow in an annual cycle and are shed, or dropped, each year. Both male and female caribou grow antlers. Growth begins from permanent knobs on their skulls. At first, the developing bone is flexible and covered with soft, hairy skin called velvet.

The blood-rich velvet nourishes the antlers until they reach full size and become hard. Then the velvet starts peeling off in strips. The peeling velvet itches, so the caribou scrapes off the rest by rubbing its antlers against trees and bushes. The "polishing" reveals shiny brown antlers. Sometimes the tips are polished nearly white.

Cows have smaller antlers than bulls. Females carry antlers most of the year, shedding them after giving birth in the spring. Then new growth begins just a few weeks later. This way, caribou mothers can use their antlers to protect themselves and their calves almost year-round.

Bull antler growth follows different timing. A bull's antler buds appear in late March and continue to grow and branch out through the summer until a thick and tall beam arches high over his head on each side. The part of the antlers that grows out over the bull's snout is called the "shovel." The biggest antlers belong to older, healthy males. Like cows, bulls use antlers to fight off predators. A bull's antlers are also a sign of power that all caribou understand.

Each bull uses its strong neck muscles and sturdy legs to shove the other male as hard as he can.

The bulls are eager to show who is the strongest. They match head-to-head with other males. Which one will win? Both grunt and dig in their hooves and push. And push! They sometimes crash together, breaking off antler tips. Most sparring matches end when one male is shoved off balance and gallops away. A few end with one or both bulls suffering serious wounds.

Sparring is a sure signal that the rut has arrived. For about two weeks in October, bulls fight to win a chance to mate. They do not gather and defend groups of females. Instead, caribou bulls travel between many groups of cows and calves, looking for females ready to mate, and chasing off other males. They stop eating and have little time to rest. By the end of the rut, most bulls are skinny and have many battle scars. They also shed their antlers at this time. Some bulls are so worn down by the rut that they do not survive the winter.

Throughout the fall, caribou travel toward their wintering grounds. Some lakes freeze so hard they can walk across them, but they must zig-zag around mountains and other barriers. The extra distance adds up. Some caribou may walk up to 3,000 miles (4,828 kilometers) in a year! Most herds reach the taiga before darkness takes over for the winter. Bulls separate into groups called bachelor herds, and cows with calves form their own small groups. All of them begin to paw the snow, digging for lichens.

Finding enough winter food is a challenge to all caribou. Peary caribou, living all year on treeless islands, graze on high ridges where the wind blows away most of the snow. Ice-crusted snow on the tundra forces most other caribou into the forests, where the soft snow is easier to dig. In mid-winter, a caribou may spend 12 hours each day digging 10 to 15 craters, to get enough to eat.

The first autumn snowfall is a sign that caribou must hurry to their wintering grounds.

Caribou compete for the best feeding spots, stealing craters by threatening with their antlers or hooves. Because cows keep their antlers all winter, they can often defend their craters from bigger bulls. Mother caribou do share their feeding holes with their young.

Calves stay with their mothers all winter. They learn where to find food and how to avoid predators. Most important, they get to know the herd's daily movements and how the patterns change with the seasons. A calf's first year is its hardest. About half of them die before their first birthday. Calves that survive often migrate to the calving grounds with their mothers, then separate into groups with other yearlings. Male calves will probably live to be about 10 years old, and females live to about 15 years.

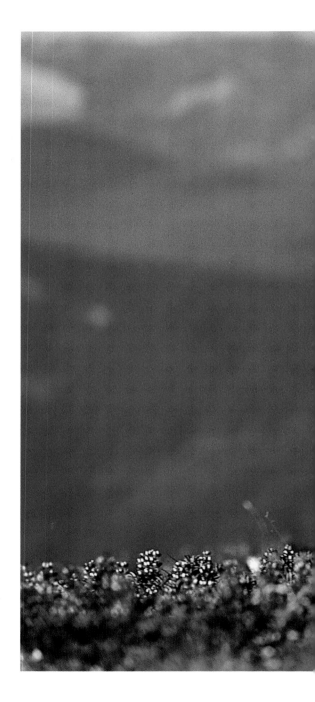

A young caribou, such as this woodland calf, learns to find food for itself mostly by watching what its mother eats at different times of the year.

Caribou require a large territory to find enough food and raise their young.
They also need a good source of clean water.

What does the future hold for caribou? The barren-ground herds sometimes grow or shrink, and no one knows exactly why. And no one is certain how to solve the problems causing Peary and woodland caribou populations to decline. But scientists understand that too much logging can damage the taiga, roads can scar the tundra, and oil exploration can disturb caribou migration. Cows with young calves are especially sensitive to changes on the land. Even more than other wild animals, caribou depend on vast, open spaces to survive.

If the Arctic wilderness is protected for caribou, they will be able to continue their spring and fall journeys across the frozen north, for generation after generation.

Caribou
FUNFACT:

Canada's 25-cent coin has a picture
of a caribou's head on one side.
The caribou is also found on postage
stamps from New Foundland and Alaska.

My POLAR ANIMALS Adventures

The date of my adventure: _____

The people who came with me: _____

_____

Where I went: _____

What polar animals I saw:

_____   _____

_____   _____

_____   _____

_____   _____

The date of my adventure: _____

The people who came with me: _____

_____

Where I went: _____

What polar animals I saw:

_____   _____

_____   _____

_____   _____

_____   _____

My POLAR ANIMALS Adventures

The date of my adventure: _____

The people who came with me: _____

_____

Where I went: _____

What polar animals I saw:

_____   _____

_____   _____

_____   _____

_____   _____

The date of my adventure: _____

The people who came with me: _____

_____

Where I went: _____

What polar animals I saw:

_____   _____

_____   _____

_____   _____

_____   _____

Explore the Fascinating World of . . .

Penguins

Cherie Winner
Illustrations by John F. McGee

PENGUINS ARE FUN TO WATCH! You may see a group of penguins shuffling along on a tall slab of ice. Suddenly one peeks over the edge, then does a kind of belly-flop into the water. In a rush, all the other penguins follow it into the sea, making a big splash.

Penguins don't fly, but they dive deeper than any other birds, walk for miles, and climb cliffs. And even though penguins are famous for living in very cold places, they actually live in more different climates than any other family of flightless birds.

There are 17 species (SPEE-sees), or kinds, of penguins. Only two, the emperors and Adelies, spend their whole life in the Antarctic, where the winter temperature can reach −76 degrees Fahrenheit (−60 degrees Celsius). The Galapagos penguin lives near the equator. There, the temperature often reaches 100 degrees Fahrenheit (37.8 degrees Celsius). The other 14 species live on shorelines in Australia, New Zealand, South America, and Africa. The climate there is similar to the climate in the northern United States.

These Adelie penguins seem to be in a hurry to go into the water.

All penguins, like these Galapagos adults, are good swimmers and divers.

Zoologists, the scientists who study animals, divide penguins into six groups: big, little, crested, banded, brush-tailed, and yellow-eyed. They all have many things in common, such as a white belly and a black or gray back. Each species also has many differences, such as the way they raise their young and the markings on the head.

The two species of big penguins are much larger than other penguins. Emperors stand about 3 feet (1 meter) tall and can weigh up to 100 pounds (45 kilograms). King penguins are about half that size. Both have bright orange or yellow on the throat and the side of the head.

Fairy penguins are the only species in the little group. They are sometimes called blue penguins because their backs are bluish. They stand about 14 inches (35 centimeters) tall and weigh 3 pounds (1.4 kilograms).

The other kinds of penguins weigh between 5 and 20 pounds (2 and 9 kilograms) and are between 17 and 27 inches (43 and 68 centimeters) tall. In all species, males are slightly bigger than females.

This pair of king penguins have found each other after being apart while feeding. Most male and female penguins look alike.

The most common species in the world is the macaroni penguin. Scientists estimate there are about 19 million of them.

Crested penguins have long yellow feathers above their eyes, like eyebrows. Rockhopper, macaroni, royal, erect-crested, Snares Island, and fiordland (fee-YORD-land) penguins belong to this group.

Banded penguins have a black stripe on their side, a white stripe on their cheek, or both. Galapagos (gul-OP-uh-gus), Humboldt, Magellanic (maj-uh-LAN-ic), and African penguins belong to this group.

Brush-tailed penguins have a longer tail than the others, and different patterns of black and white on the head. Adelie (uh-DAY-lee), chinstrap, and gentoo (jen-TOO) penguins belong to this group.

The yellow-eyed penguin has a yellowish stripe on its head. It isn't quite like any of the others and it lives mostly among shrubs and trees. It is in a group by itself.

Emperor Penguin   King Penguin   Rockhopper Penguin   Fairy Penguin

This royal is grooming, or preening, itself.
Some places are hard to reach.

All penguins have a thick coat of feathers that keeps out water and wind. Penguins need this coat to stay warm. Each penguin grooms itself for up to three hours every day keeping its feathers clean and healthy. Some species also groom their mates, and parents groom their chicks. Penguins get oil from a gland near their tail and spread it around every feather. This keeps the coat waterproof and helps protect against disease.

Their feather coat protects them from the winter chill. But in summer, penguins must cool off. They seek shady spots under a bush or in a burrow. They pant, like a dog. They hold their wings out to the side, so heat can flow away from their bodies.

Penguins are shaped like a football, plump in the middle and narrow at both ends. This shape is perfect for diving and swimming. Penguins are great at both. Penguin wings are called flippers because they are flat and stiff, like the flippers on a dolphin. Penguins swim through the water by flapping their flippers, the same way a bird flying in the air flaps its wings. They look as if they are flying underwater. Some penguins can swim as fast as 9 miles per hour (14 kilometers per hour).

Penguins spend at least half their life swimming because they only eat foods they find in the ocean. Some penguins only go a few miles out to sea. Other species swim thousands of miles to find food. Many stay at sea all winter. Fiordland penguins stay out so long, they get barnacles on their tails. Barnacles are small sea animals with hard shells that usually stick to rocks or the bottoms of ships.

After feeding, these two African penguins are heading back to their colony.

Penguins are carnivores (KAR-nuh-vorz), or meat-eaters. They consume squid, small fish such as anchovies and sardines, and tiny shrimp-like animals called krill. These sea creatures travel in huge groups called schools. When penguins find a school, they feast. One penguin can eat several pounds of food at a time. But finding these food animals, or prey (PRAY), is difficult because the schools don't stay in one place for very long. It's like having a refrigerator that is full of food but that keeps moving.

To get to where their prey are, penguins swim a few yards (meters) below the surface of the water. Sometimes they dive deeper, then they continue swimming near the surface.

When penguins find prey, they keep diving and eating for hours or even days. During one feeding trip, a gentoo penguin dove 460 times within 15 hours. It would dive, catch prey for a few minutes, come to the surface to take a breath, and then dive again.

Penguins are champion divers. They go deeper and stay underwater longer than any other birds. They usually dive 30 to 165 feet (9 to 50 meters) deep and stay down for a minute or two. But they can go 300 feet (90 meters) down and stay there for up to 6 minutes. The big penguins go even farther. The record for bird diving goes to an emperor penguin that went down 1,752 feet (535 meters) and was underwater for 18 minutes!

Penguins
FUNFACT:

Seasons in the Southern Hemisphere, where all penguins live, are the opposite of those in the Northern Hemisphere. October is early spring, and April is late fall.

This large school of fish will make a good meal
for these Galapagos penguins.

Elephant seals may peacefully share the same beach with a colony of king penguins.

Penguins hunt mainly by sight, but deep underwater, there isn't much light. Underwater, they see much better than humans. One way they find prey in the dark is by looking for flashes of bioluminescence (BY-oh-loom-ih-NESS-uns), which is light produced by animals. Many of their prey have spots that light up in the dark. These spots contain the same chemical that makes fireflies glow.

After penguins find their prey, they have to catch it. They zip one way, spin off to one side, dip and zoom and swirl in every direction. It's like an underwater dance at fast-forward speed. A trail of bubbles streams out behind them, as air that was trapped under their feathers escapes. Penguins make the prey scatter in all directions and then catch them one at a time. Because a penguin can stay underwater a long time, it might eat 100 prey on one dive.

When a penguin swallows food, it also swallows sea water. This would be poisonous for many animals, but penguins have a way to get rid of the extra salt in sea water. They have a salt gland above each eye. These glands take salt out of the penguin's blood and release it in "tears" that dribble down the penguin's bill.

When spring comes, penguins that have been at sea return to their home on land, called a colony. They go to the same colony where they were born and raised. Somehow, they know where home is.

As the penguins get closer to shore, they watch for predators (PRED-uh-torz), or enemies. Leopard seals, sea lions, and fur seals hunt for food in the water near shore, hoping to catch a plump penguin. They hide around boulders or blocks of ice in the water. Leopard seals kill more penguins than any other seal. They are quick and strong and have long, sharp teeth.

Penguins can swim for days, but they aren't fast enough to outswim these fierce predators. They need some other way of escaping harm. Traveling in a group helps, because having dozens of penguins move through the water at once can confuse a predator.

Penguins also escape by changing the way they swim. They leap out of the water like porpoises or dolphins do. This is called porpoising (POR-puhs-ing). When a penguin shoots into the air, a predator in the water can't see it. As the penguin goes back in the water, it can change direction. By the time the predator figures out where the penguin is and which direction it's going, the penguin is a long way ahead of it.

Some people think a group of swimming king penguins looks like an underwater ballet.

Once the penguins are safely on land, they may have a long trek, or journey, to reach their colony. Penguins don't look as if they would be good at walking or climbing, but they do both quite well. Emperor and Adelie penguins often cross 50 miles (80 kilometers) or more of ice to reach their colonies. They walk part of the way and "toboggan" part of the way. This means they flop on their bellies and scoot along by pushing with their feet and flippers.

Many crested penguins must climb a tall cliff to reach their colony. Rockhoppers do this by hopping up the cliff a few inches at a time. Other crested penguins use their flippers and bill to grab onto rocks or plants and pull themselves up. The trip between the water and the colony may take them more than an hour.

Some colonies have only a few hundred penguins. Others are huge. One colony of Adelie penguins covers 200 acres (80 hectares) and is home to about half a million penguins. That is the size of a field big enough to hold two shopping malls and their parking lots, with a penguin nest every few steps across the whole field.

Strong flippers make tobogganning a quick way to travel.
An emperor's long claws also help it move over the snow and ice.

Because this macaroni colony is near the water, some of the penguins are always coming from and going to the water.

Although some colonies are huge, many are shrinking. Several species of penguins are in danger of becoming extinct, or completely dying out. Thousands of penguins are killed every year by oil spilled from ships. Others cannot find enough food. Yellow-eyed penguins are the most endangered. Only about 3,000 are still living in the wild.

If you were hiking in penguin country, the first way you would know you were near a colony would be the smell. Penguin colonies really stink! All those birds leave lots of runny guano (GWON-o), or droppings, right next to their nests. Usually they don't even bother to get up. They just point their back end out of the nest, lift their tail, and the guano squirts out. Fortunately, penguins have a poor sense of smell!

If you kept walking toward the colony, you would soon hear the penguins. They are very noisy birds. They constantly honk, squawk, trumpet, and bray. Some people say they sound like donkeys. Others think they sound like elephants or squeaky gates.

Penguins recognize each other by their voices, and they always seem to have something to say. Males and females honk as they try to get a mate. They communicate with their partner as they build a nest and care for their young. They quarrel with other penguins and warn them to stay away from their nest.

Penguins
FUNFACT:

Hundreds of fairy penguins come ashore every evening near Melbourne, Australia. On Phillip Island, bleachers are set up so tourists can watch them walk up the beach to their burrows.

Most people are surprised to learn that yellow-eyed penguins don't live near snow at all, but in the forest close to the sea.

Most penguins like to be close to other penguins, but they are also protective of their own space. Every pair claims a small territory, or area, around their nest. They peck with their bills and flap their flippers at any other penguin that steps into their territory. A penguin can hit hard enough with its flipper to knock over the intruder. To help prevent fights, each nest is just far enough from its neighbors so the penguins can't reach out and peck each other.

Yellow-eyed penguins are the only ones that want privacy when they are at the colony. They nest under bushes or in burrows far enough from other members of the colony so that they can't see each other.

Penguins often keep the same mate, especially if they were successful at raising a baby, or chick, the previous year. But the partners don't travel together during the winter, so they return to the colony at different times. The male usually arrives a few days before his mate. He finds the same nest he used the year before, and starts to get it ready for the new breeding season. He cleans it and chases other penguins away. When his mate arrives, the two greet each other with loud calls. They lift their bills to the sky and flap their flippers.

A male that doesn't yet have a mate advertises that he is looking for one. He screeches and flaps his flippers. Crested penguins, for example, also shake their heads to show off their long, bright crests, or head feathers. Sometimes two penguins fight to determine which will win a mate.

Every species has its own way of making a nest and raising chicks. Some lay their eggs in a low spot on the ground, or beneath a bush. Yellow-eyed, banded, and fairy penguins make their nests among the rocks, or they dig burrows if the ground is soft. Crested penguins use grass, leaves, and twigs to make a nest on the ground.

Penguins
FUNFACT:

Yellow-eyed penguins often stay with the same mate for 10 years or more. King and emperor penguins change partners much more often. Less than one third of them choose the same partner they had the year before.

A Magellanic burrow can be quite large. The female uses it for a safe shelter to lay her eggs and care for the newborn chicks.

The white streaks around this chinstrap nest of pebbles are guano.
Sometimes the streaks are pink or green, depending on what the penguin eats.

Brush-tailed penguins build their nest out of smooth pebbles that may be about as big as a ping-pong ball. The nest is 15 to 20 inches (38 to 51 centimeters) across and several inches (centimeters) high. A good nest keeps the egg high enough to stay dry. At the start of breeding season, the colony is surrounded by snow. As the snow melts, water streams through the nests. If an egg sits in water, the chick inside will drown. The more pebbles the parents collect, the taller their nest is and the safer their baby will be. Zoologists once found a gentoo nest that contained 1,700 pebbles!

The male penguin gathers most of the pebbles. He brings them from all over. He even steals them from his neighbors' nests, when they aren't looking. Sometimes he brings his partner an especially nice pebble as a gift.

A zoologist once did an experiment at an Adelie colony. He painted a lot of pebbles bright red and left them in a pile nearby. Within a few hours, penguins close to the pile had taken some of the red pebbles to their nests. Then other penguins noticed the pretty new pebbles and started stealing them for their own nests. Within three days, the red pebbles had spread to nests all over the colony.

As the pair works on their nest, they court each other to prepare for mating. They point their bills upward and open their flippers out to the side. They bow their heads low. They sing together, although they both have harsh voices so it doesn't sound much like singing. Sometimes they use their bills to pick ticks off of each other's face and shoulders.

The partners mate and, soon, the female lays her big white eggs. King and emperor penguins lay just one egg. All other penguins lay two eggs, but they usually raise only one chick. One egg may get broken or it doesn't hatch, or the chick is small and soon dies. Penguin parents have a hard time providing enough food for one chick. They rarely find enough food for two.

The parents sit or lie on their egg to incubate it. This keeps the egg warm so the chick inside will develop, and shades it from the sun so the chick doesn't get too hot. They turn the egg many times during the day so it warms evenly on all sides.

The parents take turns incubating. One stays on the nest while the other goes back to the sea for food. The hunting parent may be gone from the nest for a few hours to three weeks. The parent that stays on the nest doesn't eat during that whole time.

When the hunting parent comes back, the two greet each other with loud calls and excited gestures. You can tell which one just came back from the sea because it looks clean, as if it had just stepped out of a bathtub. The one that has been sitting on the nest is smeared with mud and guano. They chatter and groom each other. Then they switch places. The parent that had been hunting comes onto the nest to incubate the egg, and the other one heads for the water.

Soon these gentoo eggs will hatch and the hungry chicks will constantly beg, peck, and chirp for food from their parent.

When the weather is severe, emperors may lie down and let the snow cover them until the storm passes. Each male still protects an egg on his feet.

Penguin parents almost never leave their eggs alone. If they do, the eggs will probably be eaten by predators. Hawk-like birds called skuas (SKYOO-uhz) fly over the colony looking for a chance to snatch an egg. Crabs, snakes, and foxes also eat penguin eggs.

How long the eggs incubate depends on how big the species is. Fairy penguins only incubate their eggs for 33 days. Emperor penguins incubate theirs for 64 days, the longest of any penguin.

An emperor's life is different in other ways as well. For one thing, these birds breed in winter. That's amazing, because they live in the Antarctic, where the winters are bitter cold, windy, icy, and dark.

Also, emperors do not build nests, and the male does all the incubating. As soon as the female lays her egg, she places it on the male's feet. He has a flap of loose skin on his belly that covers the egg. It warms the egg and keeps it from rolling away. The female heads out to sea for the rest of the winter. She will hunt with other females from the colony. The male stays behind for a long, hungry winter of incubating their precious egg.

All the males in the colony huddle together to stay warm. Thousands of males stand so close that each one can rest his bill on the shoulder of the bird in front of him.

For two months, the males just stand there. They chatter quietly. They take turns being on the outside of the huddle, where it is the coldest. They don't eat at all. They use their stored body fat to stay warm in the frigid wind. A male penguin that weighs 80 pounds (36 kilograms) when he begins incubating, weighs only about 40 pounds (18 kilograms) when his job is done.

The female returns about the time the egg is ready to hatch. She is fat and healthy from spending the winter at sea. She feeds the chick and keeps it warm while the male heads for the water. He will return to help care for the chick after he has eaten a lot and gained back some weight.

Hatching, or coming out of the egg, is hard work for all penguins. The chick pokes a hole in the shell with its egg tooth, a sharp spine on the tip of its bill. Sometimes it takes the chick three days to hatch. Its parents don't help at all.

The new chick is covered with soft, fluffy feathers called down. It may be light on the belly and dark on the back, or dark all over. The baby can't stand up and its eyes stay closed for a few days.

It peeps a lot, begging for food. But it may not eat right away. The parent that is with the chick often doesn't have fresh food to give it. When the other parent comes back from hunting, it feeds the chick. It regurgitates, or throws up, some food right into the chick's mouth.

Crested penguin males stay at the nest and the females do all the hunting for the chick. In other species, the parents take turns caring for their young. While one parent goes hunting for a few days or a week, the other stays with the chick to keep it warm and protect it from skuas. These birds fly just out of reach of the adult penguins' strong bills. When they see a chick that is alone, they swoop down, grab it, and quickly fly away.

Penguins
FUNFACT:

Penguin eggs have thick, tough shells that do not break easily. An emperor egg weighs nearly 1 pound (454 grams). That is eight times as much as a chicken egg!

These rockhopper chicks are still too young to have the long,
yellow "eyebrow" feathers like their parent.

This mother emperor penguin will have no trouble identifying her chick, even in such a large creche.

When chicks are several weeks old, they start to explore their habitat. In species that nest in burrows, the chicks stand outside their burrow to look around. Sometimes they gather with a few neighbor chicks. In other species, chicks leave their nests and get together in a large group called a creche (KRESH). Both parents can then go hunting at the same time.

A creche may include about 20 chicks, or as many as a few thousand. The size of the creche depends on the species and on how big the colony is. Skuas won't attack the chicks when they are in a big group like this. Huddling in a creche also helps chicks stay warm if a storm hits.

Chicks in a creche are not able to swim or hunt. They still depend on their parents for food. When an adult comes back from the sea, it calls out. Its own chick has excellent hearing and recognizes its voice and calls back. Some penguin parents run away from the creche, and the chick chases it.

They might run around for half an hour. They go many yards (meters) away from the creche, to get away from the other chicks. Finally they stop running. The parent regurgitates food for the chick. If some other chick tries to steal some of the meal, the adult slaps it with a flipper.

This is a huge rookery, another name for colony. No matter how crowded it seems, there is plenty of room for these king penguins to rest and preen their feathers.

If food is plentiful, the chicks grow quickly. After a month or two in the creche, they are almost as big as their parents. Now they are too big for skuas to carry away, and they can stay warm by themselves. They lose their down and grow sleek black-and-white coats like their parents have. This change is called fledging.

While they wait for their new coat to grow in, the chicks strengthen their swimming muscles by flapping their flippers forward and backward. They waddle closer to the water and watch adults come and go. Sometimes a big wave knocks them into the sea. Then they have to swim, whether they are ready or not!

Penguin chicks face many dangers. Even in a good year, about half the chicks in a colony die before they go to sea. Storms drown or freeze them. Skuas snatch them away. Their parents get caught in an oil spill or have trouble finding food. In one very bad year, only one gentoo chick survived in a colony of 3,000 families.

More young die when they first go into the water. They don't swim well yet, and they don't know about the dangerous predators near shore. Sea lions and leopard seals catch many of them.

Penguins
FUNFACT:

Most birds have air spaces in their bones, to make them lighter so they can fly. Penguin bones are solid and heavy, to help the penguins dive deep in the water.

Adelies normally lay two eggs but often one does not survive. This parent has two chicks to feed. The parents take turns bringing food to their hungry young.

These king penguins have gathered in the colony
while they wait to molt their feathers.

Young penguins that survive all these dangers join a group of adults. They are on their own now, and must find and catch their own food. Their parents have gone to sea to find food and gain back the weight they lost while rearing their chicks.

Soon the adults return to the colony to molt, or replace their feathers. All of their old, tattered feathers fall out, a few at a time, and new ones grow in their place. This takes a huge amount of energy. It also takes a long time, from 2 to 4 weeks in smaller species, and 4 to 6 weeks in bigger ones. The chicks, which just got their first coat of adult feathers, will not molt until the next year.

Molting is a hard time for the penguins. They don't eat. They don't even chatter much. Their tender skin would bruise or tear if they fought with a neighbor. So they just stand quietly as their new coat of feathers grows.

The adults are skinny and hungry when they finish molting. Then they head out to sea once more.

Emperors normally never set foot on dry land. The only time they come out of the sea is to ride on floating sea ice or breed and raise their young on the ice of Antarctica.

These kings are as much at home in the sea as any dolphin or whale.
If they are away from the colony on a long food hunt, they even sleep on the water.

Soon the air turns cold and the days grow short. Some species, like Galapagos and yellow-eyed penguins, stay near their colony all winter. They go on short hunting trips and return home within a few days. Others, like emperors and Magellanic penguins, swim the open sea all winter. They hunt and eat and grow fat hundreds of miles from the colony. They may not touch land for months. When they need to rest, they float at the surface of the water like ducks. They travel with other members of their colony, but they may not see their mates until spring, when they go home to raise a new chick.

Many young from the year before also return to the colony, but they aren't ready to breed yet. Some wait until they are 9 years old. In the meantime, they learn how to mate and raise chicks by watching the older birds.

That seems like a long time to wait before raising offspring of their own, but wild penguins can live for about 20 years. Those young birds will be part of a crowded, noisy, smelly, thriving penguin colony for many years to come.

Penguins
FUNFACT:

Some penguin colonies are more than 4,000 years old, some are about 100 years old, and others are nearly new. Gentoos move to a fresh place every few years.

My POLAR ANIMALS Adventures

The date of my adventure: _____

The people who came with me: _____

_____

Where I went: _____

What polar animals I saw:

_____   _____

_____   _____

_____   _____

_____   _____

The date of my adventure: _____

The people who came with me: _____

_____

Where I went: _____

What polar animals I saw:

_____   _____

_____   _____

_____   _____

_____   _____

My POLAR ANIMALS Adventures

The date of my adventure: _____

The people who came with me: _____

_____

Where I went: _____

What polar animals I saw:

_____   _____

_____   _____

_____   _____

_____   _____

The date of my adventure: _____

The people who came with me: _____

_____

Where I went: _____

What polar animals I saw:

_____   _____

_____   _____

_____   _____

Explore the Fascinating World of . . .

Polar Bears

Linda Tagliaferro
Illustrations by John F. McGee

POLAR BEARS are cool animals. But it's not just because they are fun to learn about. Polar bears live in the coastal areas of the Arctic—the areas around the North Pole—at the top of the world. These are lands of snow, ice, and freezing cold water. There are heavy snowstorms, freezing temperatures, and cold, harsh winds in these lands. Very few animals could survive in places like this, but to the polar bear, this area is a comfortable home.

The mighty polar bear is the largest meat eater that lives on land.

Two polar bear cubs, or babies, follow their mother closely. Female polar bears give birth about every three years.

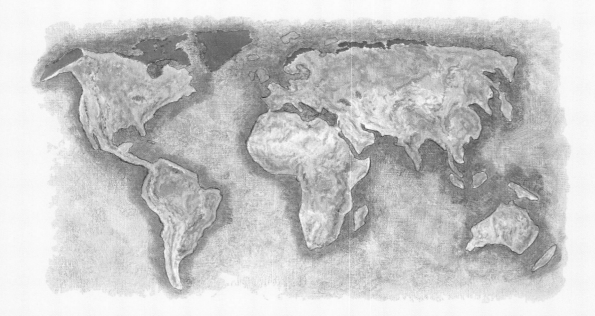

There are areas in five countries in the far north where polar bears roam: Alaska in the United States, the northern part of Canada, Greenland (an island owned by Denmark), some islands in Norway, and Russia.

These amazing bears are the largest members of the bear family. Only Alaskan brown bears can sometimes grow as big as polar bears. There are eight species (SPEE-sees), or kinds, of bears, and some scientists think that the polar bear is the most recent to develop. Some scientists think that the polar bears are the distant relatives of the brown bears that lived in an area near Siberia (sy-BEER-ee-uh) in eastern Russia.

Polar bears are also the largest carnivores (KAR-nuh-vorz), or meat eaters, on land. The males can stand up to 10 feet (3 meters) tall on their hind legs. That's taller than a school bus! Males can weigh over 1,000 pounds (454 kilograms). Adult females are much smaller than the males and can be about 6 to 8 feet (1.8 to 2.4 meters) tall. That's still bigger than a tall basketball player! Female polar bears weigh about 500 pounds (227 kilograms).

These mighty animals have shorter arms and legs than other bears, but they have tremendously strong muscles. Their heads and ears are smaller than most bears', and they only have a very small tail. Larger ears and tails would stick out and get cold quickly in the freezing Arctic climate. The polar bear's ears are rounded and have fur on the inside to protect against the cold. It's like having built-in earmuffs!

Polar bears stand on their hind legs to get a better view or to pick up the scent of food. They can even walk on two legs for short distances.

Polar bears like to curl up when they sleep to keep warm. They sleep about 7 or 8 hours at a time, just like humans, and they also take short naps during the day to conserve energy.

In the winter when hunting is good, a polar bear might gain over 200 pounds (90 kilograms). In the summer when food is scarce, it will get its energy from all the fat that it has stored.

Temperatures in the Arctic can go down as low as -50 degrees Fahrenheit (-45 degrees Celsius) in the winter. Luckily for the polar bear, its body is well built for survival in cold weather. In order to keep warm, the polar bear has a "coat" of thick white fur. There are actually two layers of fur. The lower layer is like thick, oily wool, and the top hairs are long and hollow. They keep the bear warm by holding in some air like a fluffy down comforter.

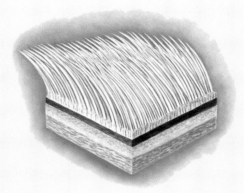

The bear's white fur helps it to blend into the snow and ice. But its fur is actually colorless. The bear's fur looks white because it reflects the light from the sun. Sometimes, the bear's fur looks yellowish-white because the sunlight has changed its color. The polar bear's skin is all black, but it can't be seen because of all its fur. The dark color helps to hold in the heat from sunlight. The eyes, nose, and tongue of the polar bear are also black.

Another reason that polar bears keep warm in the cold is because they have a layer of blubber, or fat, inside their bodies. The layer of blubber can be as thick as 4½ inches (11.5 centimeters). To keep this layer of fat, a polar bear must eat fatty foods, like one seal a week. A polar bear can eat about 100 pounds (45.3 kilograms) of blubber at just one meal. That's like a 90-pound (40.8 kilogram) human child eating 9 pounds (4 kilograms) of animal fat for dinner!

Polar Bear
FUNFACT:

The scientific name for the polar bear, *Ursus maritimus*, means "sea bear" in Latin.

A polar bear's inside layer of blubber helps to keep it warm
when it swims in icy waters.

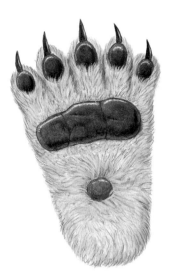

The bear's paws are very large and look like big furry slippers. The front paws are round and a little larger than its long back paws. The front paws are about 12 inches (30.5 centimeters) wide. That's bigger than a school notebook! These big paws are used as powerful weapons for attacking the bear's prey (PRAY)—the animals that it kills for food. There are black pads that are as rough as sandpaper on the bottom of all of its paws. These coarse pads, together with the thick white fur on the bottom of the bear's feet, help to keep it from slipping on the ice and snow. There are also small bumps on the bottom of the bear's paws to help it get a good grip on the ice.

The polar bear's front paws are webbed like ducks' feet. These paws act like flippers and help the bear to swim. These Arctic bears are just as comfortable on land as they are in the water. They are excellent swimmers and can even stay underwater for a minute or two. They sometimes need to swim to get where they want to go. In the summer when the ice begins to melt, polar bears may get stuck out on a floating piece of ice. Then they have to jump in the water and swim to shore. They can swim at a speed of 6 miles per hour (9.6 kilometers per hour), and can dive as deep as 15 feet (4.5 meters) below the water's surface. Their long necks help them to keep their heads out of the icy water as they paddle along.

On land a polar bear usually walks slowly—about 3 miles per hour (4.8 kilometers per hour). It can run up to 25 miles per hour (40 kilometers per hour), but it gets tired quickly. Because it has thick fur on the outside and a layer of blubber on the inside, the polar bear overheats, or gets too hot, if it runs fast.

To survive in the Arctic, polar bears must be good hunters. They have longer snouts than most bears, and they have a superb sense of smell. They sometimes hold their noses high in the air or stand on their hind legs to sniff the air for prey, which can be miles away. Their eyesight is sharp, and their hearing is also excellent.

They have longer, sharper teeth than other bears. This is important because they are meat eaters. Their claws are sharp and curved and hold tightly onto their prey. There are five claws on each of the polar bear's paws, and they can be 2 inches (5 centimeters) long. The claws also make it easier to walk on the slippery ice.

A mother polar bear and her two cubs sniff the air.
They can smell a seal more than 1 mile (1.6 kilometers) away.

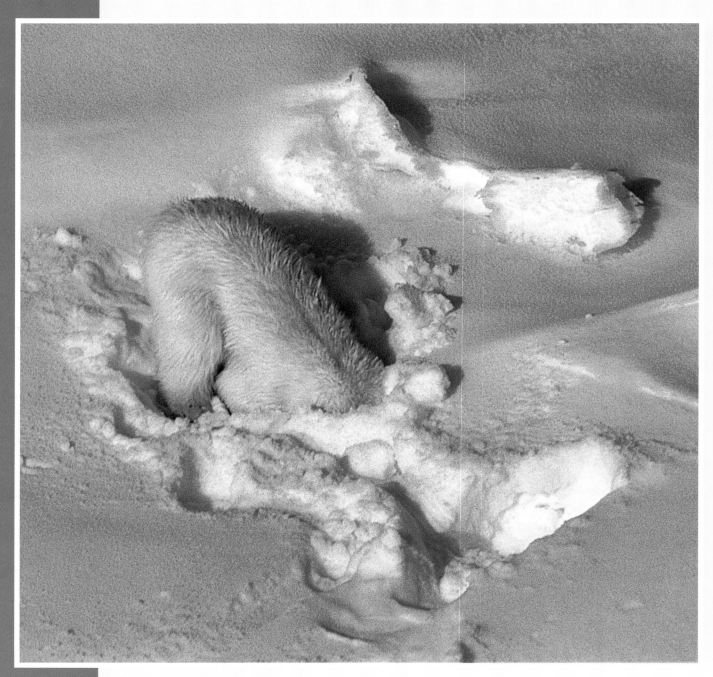

A polar bear tramples the snow and digs deep
to hunt for a ringed seal pup.

Polar bears eat more meat than any other bears. They have extra-large stomachs to help them digest their meals. The polar bear's favorite food is a type of seal called the ringed seal. It is the smallest seal in the Arctic and measures about 4 feet (1.2 meters) in length. An average ringed seal weighs about 150 pounds (68 kilograms). They are plump because they have a thick layer of blubber under their skin. Ringed seals swim in the cold Arctic waters, but they have to come up for air. The seals use the sharp nails on their flippers to scratch out holes in the ice. They swim up to these openings, called breathing holes, and poke their heads up for air every 5 to 15 minutes. This is when polar bears try to catch them with one quick swipe of their powerful paws.

If the polar bears are very quiet, the seals may not hear them, or see them, because the bears are camouflaged (KAM-uh-flajd) against the white snow. Since their fur is the same color, it blends into the background and makes the bears hard to see. The seals have many different breathing holes, so they might not use one right away. The polar bears must be patient. They may have to wait for hours before a ringed seal appears. But even when a seal appears, it might hear or catch sight of the bear at the last minute and escape by swimming under the ice. A polar bear might only be successful in 1 out of 20 hunts.

After catching a seal, a polar bear eats only the skin and fat and leaves the rest of the meat. Scavengers (SKAV-in-jers), any animals that look for leftover food, usually eat the remains of the bear's meal. Arctic foxes, for example, sometimes follow a polar bear after its hunt. They wait until the bear is finished with its meal and then feast on the seal meat that is left over. Young bears that are not as successful at hunting may also join in. Arctic birds like ravens and Ivory gulls then finish off any meat that is left on the seal's bones.

Polar bears also eat the rich blubber of walruses, but they must fight hard for this food. Some adult male walruses may weigh up to 3,000 pounds (1,360 kilograms), and they can injure or kill a polar bear by attacking it with their enormous, dangerous tusks. Usually the bears only succeed at catching young, small walruses. Sometimes they might find a dead adult walrus on the ice.

Arctic foxes closely follow a polar bear,
hoping to get the remains of a successful hunt.

Polar bears prefer to hunt by sitting and waiting because they overheat quickly when they run.

In order to hunt for seals, polar bears need to wait on the ice. In the Arctic summer, some of the ice melts and this makes it hard for the bears to catch their food. The seals are usually farther out in the water. So at this time, polar bears eat what they can. They look for birds like snow geese or eat their eggs. They use their sharp sense of smell to locate the carcasses (KAR-kus-iz), or dead bodies, of whales, fish, or other animals that have washed up on the ice. If they are very hungry in the summer, they may eat berries and plants that they find on land. They may even eat tiny lemmings, small Arctic animals that look like mice with short tails. Sometimes they do not eat for several months.

A mother bear watches out for her cubs while they eat food that she hunted for the three of them. The mother bear must eat enough to produce milk for her growing cubs.

Scientists can tell what kind of food a polar bear has just eaten by looking at its droppings, or scat. Sometimes there will be fur from a ringed seal in the bear's scat.

A polar bear may seem like a sloppy eater, getting blood and fat all over its fur as it feeds. But when it's finished eating, it spends time cleaning itself. It might wash itself by jumping in the water, or it might lick itself clean in much the same way that a cat does. This neatness isn't just to make the polar bear's fur look good. If the polar bear's fur gets wet or matted down with dirt, it can't protect against the cold. The fur needs to stand up straight so it can trap the air and hold the heat in. The fur needs to stay as clean as possible at all times.

This polar bear shakes itself off after a swim.
Polar bears also drag themselves across the ice to dry off.

These adult polar bears gather in Churchill, Manitoba, in Canada. The town is known as "The Polar Bear Capital of the World" because every October and November many polar bears go there to wait for the ice to freeze over.

The polar bear is a wanderer. In the summer when the ice begins to melt, some bears travel north where the weather is colder and there is more ice. Then they go south in the winter as the ice begins to freeze again. During the coldest months, the polar bear must eat a great deal and put on a lot of weight. If not, it could starve to death during the warm months when food is scarce. The extra weight acts like fuel for the bear's body when it can't find enough food to eat.

During their migration (my-GRAY-shun), or moving from one area to another, polar bears may travel hundreds or even thousands of miles. But they usually go back to the places where they learned to hunt when they were cubs, or baby bears. This is called their territory, or home range. A polar bear's home range is much larger than the ranges of any other kind of bear. They might be anywhere from 20,000 square miles (51,000 square kilometers) to 135,000 square miles (350,650 square kilometers). Even though home ranges might overlap, polar bears do not fight over their territories.

Polar bears usually travel alone, but in some places, like Churchill in Manitoba, Canada, large groups of polar bears gather around Hudson Bay in the late fall. They are waiting for the weather to get colder. Then when the water freezes, the polar bears roam the ice looking for seals that come up at breathing holes.

Polar Bear
FUNFACT:

The powerful jaws of polar bears have 42 teeth to grip their prey. Adult humans have 32 teeth.

Polar bears look ferocious, but they can be quite playful with each other. They can grab hold of each other and wrestle, but they are not trying to hurt one another. They are just having fun! This also helps to prepare them for real fighting. If another polar bear attacks them, they will know the right moves to defend themselves. They also learn from play-fighting which other bears are too strong for them. They will keep away from them in a real fight.

When a polar bear wants to play, it shakes its head from side to side to let another bear know it is in the mood for a fighting game. Both young bears and adult bears play. They might stand up on their hind legs, with their front paws down and their chins next to their chests, to get ready to tackle another playful bear.

Even though polar bears can be playful, there are times when they are very serious. There is no mistaking a bear that is not in the mood for play. Growling, roaring, and hissing warn other bears that they should stay away. When a polar bear lowers its head and lays its ears back, it is also a sign that it's not in a good mood.

These two adult male polar bears are play-fighting.
This does not hurt the bears, and it teaches them real fighting skills
they will need later to compete for females.

Polar bears have long necks, and their front legs are much longer than their back legs.

Bears also have ways of showing each other good manners, too. If a large bear is eating, a younger or smaller one might want the leftovers. A well-mannered young bear gets low to the ground and silently comes close to the larger bear who is eating. Then, the smaller bear quietly circles around the food. It shyly begs for food by gently touching noses with the dining bear and often gets what it wants if it acts politely in this way.

In the spring, usually in April or May, female polar bears give off a scent in their urine that tells the male bears that they are ready to mate. With their sharp sense of smell, many of the males follow the females. The eager males fight to see who is the strongest, and only this one earns the right to mate with the female. The winning male and the female stay together for about a week, but then the female's scent changes. She ignores the male, and he goes off, looking for another female that is ready to mate.

An angry polar bear growls to warn other bears to stay far away.

This hole in the snow shows where a mother bear and her cubs came out of their den. There is a short tunnel and usually one main room, but sometimes there can be two, or even four smaller rooms in the den.

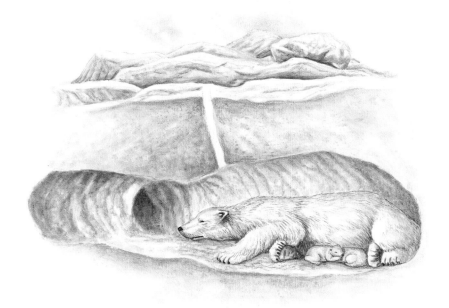

The female bear prepares to give birth to her cubs, or baby bears. She must eat a great deal of food in the next few months. She needs to build up enough fat to last for a long time. She will not be eating for many months, and she might lose half of her weight in that time. In the late fall, she looks for a safe place to dig a den. She usually finds a place that provides some shelter against the raging Arctic winds. To keep out the cold, she digs a long tunnel that leads to a den, which is a resting area. This is the place where she goes into a kind of sleep while her babies develop inside her. She does not eat or drink, or pass water or waste during this time. The den is only about 4 feet (1.2 meters) across and 3 feet (less than a meter) high at the center.

While other types of bears go into hibernation (hi-ber-NAY-shun), which is a long, deep winter sleep, male polar bears do not. They continue to roam around their home range all winter. Although mother polar bears go into a kind of sleep in their den, it is not as deep a sleep as in hibernation. They can wake up more quickly than truly hibernating bears if they sense danger.

A bear cub rests inside its den. Polar bear mothers often dig dens in snowdrifts on mountains to keep warm and far from male bears that can sometimes be dangerous to cubs.

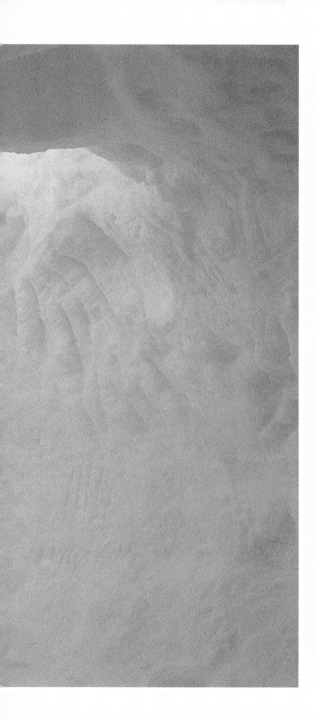

In the winter as the mother bear sleeps, her cubs are born 8 months after she mated. Usually, two cubs are born at the same time, and on rare occasions, three may be born.

At birth, the cubs are only about as big as a kitten, and they weigh about 1 pound (about 0.5 kilogram). They have pink bodies with just a thin coat of short, white hair. Their eyes are closed, and they can't see or hear. They are born without teeth. The cubs depend on their mother for food and warmth. But even though their mother is sleeping, she is still providing for them. Her rich, fatty milk helps them to grow quickly. In just the first month after their birth, the cubs can grow to more than four times their birth weight. At this time, they can open their eyes and see. They can also hear, but they still aren't able to walk around.

By the time that it is two months old, a polar bear cub may be as big as a human baby. Now it has teeth, and it has grown thick white fur. It can walk around in the den by itself, but it is still not strong enough to go out into the harsh surroundings in the outside world. The den is much warmer than the outside air. In the spring when they are about 3 months old, the cubs are ready to come out of the den with their mother. They stay around the den for about 12 days or more, and they sleep there at night.

Staying near the den for this time helps the cubs get used to the cold weather outside and gives them practice walking around in the ice and snow.

The female polar bear is a very good mother. She protects her cubs fiercely if there is danger. Even though females are smaller than male polar bears, a mother bear will lower her head and charge at a male bear that threatens her cubs. She has good reason to do this. Male bears sometimes kill the helpless cubs.

Polar Bear
FUNFACT:

During very severe snowstorms, a polar bear might dig a small hole in the snow. It curls up in this cozy space until the storm passes.

This mother polar bear defends her cubs from an approaching male.
Even though female polar bears are smaller than males, their fierce
behavior usually scares males away from their young.

This mother polar bear is feeding milk to her two cubs. Even though they have thick fur, the cubs do not have an inside layer of fat yet. They need their mother's milk for energy and to keep warm.

There are many dangers in the cold north, such as starvation, disease, and attacks by other animals. Many cubs do not live past their first year. For two or three years, the cubs drink their mother's milk, and they begin to eat meat that their mother has hunted. She must hunt well in order to be able to produce enough food for herself and her cubs.

The cubs stay by their mother's side and learn how to survive in the harsh conditions of the Arctic. Together, the mother bear and her cubs travel down to the sea ice to look for seals to eat. They stop several times a day to rest or for the mother bear to nurse her cubs. The mother digs small shelters in the snow where the cubs can sleep safely.

If the mother bear senses danger and wants her cubs to come to her immediately, she gives out a soft growl to get their attention. They learn how to hunt for ringed seals by watching her as she skillfully catches the plump animals. Sometimes the cubs even help her hunt. The cubs might sit at nearby seal breathing holes. They may not be swift enough or strong enough to catch a seal that needs to come up for air. But if the seal sees them, it may come up for air in another breathing hole, possibly one where the mother bear is waiting.

The mother bear hunts for seal pups as well as adult ringed seals. The pups are born in April or May, and they are called whitecoats. They live in places called birth lairs. This is a covered den under the snow. Polar bears can smell them even if they can't see them under the snow. When the mother bear finds one of these birth lairs, she smashes its roof with her powerful paws and sticks her head into the enclosure to catch the seals inside.

When the cubs have reached the age of 2 or 3, the mother chases them away or abandons them. Now they are all alone and must take care of themselves. If they have learned all the survival skills from their mother, they will be able to hunt successfully on their own. They may travel over 600 miles (965 kilometers) to establish a new home range that is far from their mother's. If they can make it on their own until they are 5 or 6 years old, they will be ready to mate and have families of their own. At the age of 10 or 11, they will reach their adult weight. In the wild, polar bears usually live from 15 to 20 years.

Polar Bear
FUNFACT:

Polar bears do the "dog paddle" when they swim. Their front paws and arms propel them through the water while their back legs and feet lay flat and help them to steer into the direction they want to go.

Polar bear cubs learn to hunt and swim by imitating their mother.

A one-year-old cub follows in its mother's footsteps. Although adult bears can run as fast as a horse, they normally walk slowly to avoid overheating or to allow their cubs to keep up with them.

Scientists who study polar bears in the wild estimate that there are between 22,000 and 25,000 currently living in the Arctic. But there are some serious threats to the bears' existence. Some animals are considered endangered species. This means that they are in danger of dying out forever. Fortunately, the polar bear is not an endangered species. But it is considered a threatened species. This means that there are some problems that might lead to its becoming endangered.

Polar Bear
FUNFACT:

The native Inuit people who live in the Arctic call the polar bear "Nanook."

This polar bear cub stands on its hind legs because it is curious, but it stays close to its mother to keep safe and warm.

This polar bear is cooling off on the ice. Polar bears also spread out and crawl on their stomachs to avoid breaking the ice when it is very thin.

Every year the Earth's temperature is rising a little bit. This is known as global warming. The rate of warming is at least twice as fast in the Arctic as it is in other parts of the world. This means that the ice is getting thinner and there is less of it than there was in the past.

Because the polar bear needs the ice as a place to hunt seals and other prey, global warming might cause some bears to starve to death. In Canada especially, scientists have found that more and more polar bear cubs are dying from lack of food.

This polar bear cub follows its mother in the snow. Most female
polar bears are 5 or 6 years old when they give birth to their first cubs.

Some bears in places like Churchill, Manitoba, in Canada have even roamed through town where people live. The hungry bears look for food in garbage dumps. Sometimes people have to capture them and bring them back into the wild.

Pollution (puh-LOO-shun) is another threat to polar bears. Poisonous chemicals called PCBs have found their way into the food supply of polar bears.

Another threat to polar bears is the impact that humans can have on their habitat. The Arctic National Wildlife Refuge was created in 1960 in Alaska as a protected wild area. This is one important area where mother polar bears build their dens to protect them and their newborn cubs.

This place in Alaska is rich in oil. Some people want to drill for oil in this area. But mother polar bears are very sensitive to the noise of humans. This could cause them to leave their dens or abandon their cubs. If people are allowed to drill for oil, they must be very careful to protect these bears.

Fortunately, there are people who are working to protect polar bears. Hopefully, this will help the bears to survive so there will be more of these wonderful Arctic animals in the wild.

Polar Bear
FUNFACT:

The polar bear's body temperature is 98.6 degrees Fahrenheit (37 degrees Celsius)—the same as that of humans.

My POLAR ANIMALS Adventures

The date of my adventure: _____

The people who came with me: _____

_____

Where I went: _____

What polar animals I saw:

_____   _____

_____   _____

_____   _____

_____   _____

The date of my adventure: _____

The people who came with me: _____

_____

Where I went: _____

What polar animals I saw:

_____   _____

_____   _____

_____   _____

_____   _____

My POLAR ANIMALS Adventures

The date of my adventure: _____

The people who came with me: _____

_____

Where I went: _____

What polar animals I saw:

_____   _____

_____   _____

_____   _____

_____   _____

The date of my adventure: _____

The people who came with me: _____

_____

Where I went: _____

What polar animals I saw:

_____   _____

_____   _____

_____   _____

_____   _____

Explore the Fascinating World of . . .

Seals

Wayne Lynch
Illustrations by John F. McGee

OCEANS COVER almost three-quarters of the surface of the Earth. Because the oceans are so large and filled with food, it is no surprise that many mammals live there. These mammals, called marine mammals, include giant whales, fast-swimming dolphins and porpoises, and plant-munching manatees, which some people call sea cows. There are other marine mammals too, such as fuzzy-faced sea otters, great white polar bears, and pinnipeds (PIN-a-peds). The name pinniped means fin-footed. The pinnipeds are a large group of marine mammals that are commonly known as seals. Everyone can identify a seal, but most don't know that there are 33 species (SPEE-sees), or kinds, of seals. That's a large number of seals to remember. Luckily, all of the seals belong to just three different groups. It is easy to figure out which group a seal belongs to simply by looking at the animal's ears and watching how it swims and moves on land.

There are only about 1300 Hawaiian monk seals, making it one of the rarest seals on Earth.

This crabeater seal in Antarctica is a lucky one. The scars on its side are from an old leopard seal attack.

This southern elephant seal is molting its old skin.
It throws damp sand over its body to help it cool off.

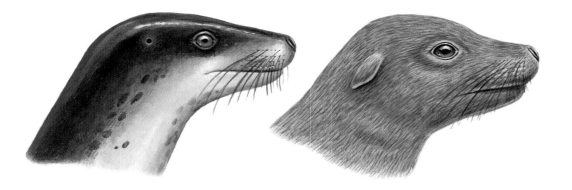

The seals in one group have no external ears, just a small hole on each side of their head through which they hear. Because they appear to have no ears, they are often called the earless seals. This group includes the harp seal, the ringed seal, and the bearded seal. All of the earless seals swim by sweeping their large rear flippers, which are shaped like a fan, from side to side to propel themselves through the water. On land these seals either drag themselves forward by using the strong claws on their small front flippers, or they hump along the ground like a giant caterpillar. Usually the earless seals do not move very fast, nor very far from the water.

This southern elephant seal pup is snoozing on a beach in southern Argentina. The pup will stay on shore for 50 days after its mother abandons it.

A large male California sea lion tries to herd a female into his territory along the beach. The female barks in protest.

The second group of seals is made up of sea lions and fur seals, including Hooker's sea lion, the California sea lion, and the northern fur seal. Sea lions are the seals that circus people train to balance a ball on the end of their nose. All sea lions and fur seals have small curled ear flaps, and they are commonly called the eared seals. Eared seals swim differently than the earless seals. Instead of swimming with their rear flippers, they use their broad front flippers, which are shaped like the blade of a canoe paddle, and they use their rear flippers to steer. On land the eared seals use their rear flippers to walk and run around, and they can do this better than all the other seals. When an Antarctic fur seal is frightened or angry, it can run almost as fast as a human.

The third group of seals includes only one seal, the walrus. This is the easiest seal to recognize because it is the only one that has two long white teeth called tusks. A large pair of tusks on an adult male walrus can be as long as a child's baseball bat, about 26 inches (65 centimeters) long. In the water, the walrus uses both its front and rear flippers to swim. On land, it walks by using its rear flippers in the same way as a fur seal or sea lion, but much slower.

Seals
FUNFACT:

Seals, like many other animals, need several years to grow up before they can mate and raise a family. Most female seals are mature at age four, whereas most male seals don't mate until they are five to seven years of age.

Seals live in all the oceans of the world. Some, such as fur seals and the sea lions of the Galapagos Islands, live in the hot tropics and swim with sea turtles and marine iguanas. Other seals and sea lions live along the Atlantic and the Pacific coasts of the United States and Canada, where it is warm in the summer and cold in the winter. But the greatest number of seals live in the Arctic and the Antarctic, the coldest places on Earth, where winter temperatures often dip below -40 degrees Fahrenheit (-40 degrees Celsius). In the Arctic and the Antarctic, the surface of the ocean may be frozen all year round. Even when the ice melts, the water is still very cold and below the freezing point of 29 degrees Fahrenheit (-1.6 degrees Celsius). Water drains heat from an animal's body much faster than air does, and staying warm in the water is one of the biggest problems that a seal faces. How do most seals stay warm? The answer is blubber. Blubber is a thick layer of fat that forms a blanket under the seal's skin everywhere on its body. On a large blubbery walrus or elephant seal, the fat under its skin may be 4 inches (10 centimeters) thick. That is thicker than a triple cheeseburger!

The Antarctic fur seal has brownish-gray fur as do many eared
seals, but some, such as the Australian sea lion, have more silvery-gray fur,
and the fur of the female South American sea lion is pale gold in color.

When a walrus gets overheated, it must climb over its buddies
to reach the water. As it does, the grumpy sunbathers usually
jab him with tusks to hurry him along.

All seals have some fur, but unlike the fur on most other animals, the fur on a seal's body does not help it stay warm in the water. The fur on most seals is too thin to keep them warm, and their skin gets soaked as soon as they dive into the water. However, the fur seals are different. They have one of the thickest fur coats of any mammal. It is so thick that water never soaks through to the animal's skin, and the seal stays warm even in very cold water.

Seals leave the water to rest and to have their young. When they do, they may overheat because of the thick fat or dense fur covering their body. How do seals stay cool? Some pant like a dog to cool themselves, while other seals wave their flippers around like a fan. When a walrus overheats, its skin turns red like a cooked lobster, and it must dive back into the cold water to cool off.

All seals are carnivores (KAR-nuh-vorz) and eat other animals when they are hungry. The three most common foods they eat are fish, squid, and a shrimp-like animal called krill. Scientists can sometimes find out what a seal has been eating by checking the color of its scat, or droppings. When a seal eats fish, its droppings are often grayish white. When it eats krill, its droppings are pink, and when it eats squid, its droppings are yellow.

Seals
FUNFACT:

The smallest seal in the world, the female Galapagos fur seal, weighs just 60 pounds (27 kilograms). The largest seal, the male southern elephant seal, weighs as much as 11,000 pounds (4990 kilograms).

One seal, the leopard seal of Antarctica, feeds on krill and fish in the winter, but then switches to penguins in the summer. The swift, powerful leopard seal hunts penguins in several different ways. One way is to stalk, or follow, the birds from under thin ice. With this method, an underwater seal follows a bird walking across newly formed ice, breaks through the ice—which can be 3 inches (7.5 centimeters) thick—and grabs the unsuspecting bird. If a penguin spots a leopard seal before it attacks, the bird will freeze with fear until it feels safe enough to continue, sometimes even for over an hour.

A leopard seal can also leap onto ice floes and snatch any careless penguin that is standing near the edge. If a penguin is not close enough to catch, the seal may try to drive the birds off the safety of the ice then pursue them in an underwater chase.

A female seal, such as this ringed seal, is called a "cow," a male is a "bull," a newborn is a "pup," and the area where the seals gather to mate is called a "rookery."

Another hunting method for a leopard seal is to hide between pieces of floating ice near shore. When the penguins return from a fishing trip and head to land, they may swim into the seal's deadly jaws. The most common technique is for a leopard seal to patrol an ice edge where the penguins must leap up out of the water onto the ice in order to reach shore. When the tide is out, the ice edge may be 5 feet (1.5 meters) high and the birds may have to make many leaps before they succeed. Tired penguins are easy targets.

The bearded seal, like all seals, is shaped like a torpedo.
This helps it to move through the water more easily.

159

Sea lions like to play underwater, circling and
chasing each other as these Australian sea lions are doing.

All seals are expert divers, and all of them can hold their breath for at least 20 minutes or more. Most humans cannot hold their breath for even one minute. What happens inside humans' bodies when they stop breathing? Actually, nothing much changes at all. Their temperature stays the same, their heart keeps beating, and their blood continues to move around inside their bodies as usual. But one important thing does change as humans hold their breath. The oxygen in their blood slowly burns away, and if the oxygen level gets too low, they faint.

When human scuba divers go underwater they carry extra oxygen with them inside tanks strapped to their backs. A seal also carries extra oxygen, but in a different way than a scuba diver. A seal has twice as much blood in its body as a human does, so it can carry more oxygen. A seal also stores extra oxygen in its muscles. Seal meat is black in color for this reason. With so much extra oxygen, a seal can dive for many minutes without breathing.

Two other things happen inside a seal's body that do not happen inside a human when it holds its breath. When a seal dives, its heart slows down and blood flows only to the animal's heart and brain. Very little blood circulates to the rest of its body. In this way, the seal saves the oxygen for the two most important parts of its body, the main engine (the heart) and the central computer (the brain). This allows it to stay underwater even longer.

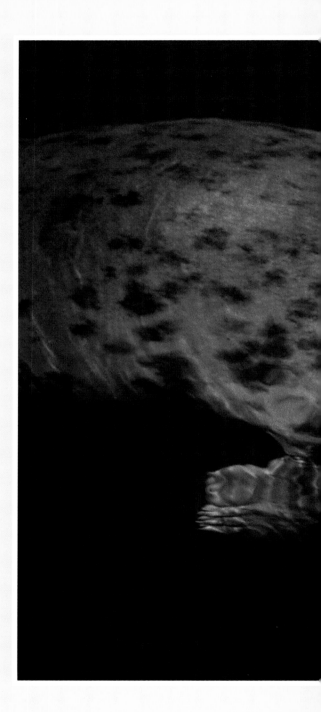

Most seals can hunt day or night. Even during the day, some seals dive so deeply that no sunlight reaches them, and the water is as black as a moonless night. In the darkness of the deep ocean, a seal depends upon its special eyes and whiskers to find its prey (PRAY), the animals it hunts for food. The eyes of a seal are very large to collect as much light as possible. Seals also have a shiny layer on the back of their eyes that magnifies light. Many land mammals such as cats, dogs, and deer have a similar reflective layer in their eyes, called the tapetum lucidum (ta-PEE-tum LOO-si-dum), which shines brightly at night when they stare at the headlights of a car.

Seals
FUNFACT:

All seals dive, but the best divers are the two biggest seals, the northern and southern elephant seals. One northern elephant seal was recorded diving underwater for two hours, and it reached a depth of 5500 feet (1676 meters).

Most seals, including this gray seal, have cone-shaped teeth
to help them hold slippery, wiggling prey.

The whiskers on a seal also help it to locate prey in the darkness. A walrus, the most whiskery of the seals, has over 600 thick, stiff whiskers on its floppy upper lip. It uses its whiskers like fingers to feel for sea cucumbers, worms, clams, and crabs hidden in the mud on the ocean bottom. Other seals use their whiskers to detect vibrations in the water when a fish or squid swims nearby. The Antarctic fur seal has only 40 to 60 sensitive whiskers, but some of them may be 18 inches (46 centimeters) long, which is as long as a child's arm.

A walrus never uses its tusks to dig for food.
Instead it uses them to defend itself, chop holes
in the ice, and to haul itself out of the water.

Newborn northern fur seals have black fur when they are born.
Neighboring pups often cluster together when their mothers leave to go fishing.

For most of the year, seals are scattered over the oceans, traveling alone or in small groups. The spring breeding season is the one time of the year when many of them come together in crowds to find a partner. Twenty of the 33 species of seals breed on land (land-breeding seals), while the rest breed on the ice (ice-breeding seals). The seals that breed on land, such as fur seals and sea lions, form the largest groups, or colonies. Millions of Antarctic fur seals may crowd together on the beaches of a single island. A remote island is a good place for a seal colony to gather because there are usually no bears, wolves, humans, or other predators (PRED-uh-tors), animals that hunt other animals for food, to disturb them.

Seals
FUNFACT:

The most threatened seals in the world are the two monk seals: the Hawaiian monk seal and the Mediterranean monk seal, both of which number less than 2000 individuals.

Young southern elephant seals begin to fight when they are less than a year old.
This is serious business and only one in ten adult males will ever grow up to be a father.

Wherever large numbers of land-breeding seals get together, the males usually fight with each other to win female partners. Males, or bulls, chase, wrestle, and slash and tear each other with their sharp teeth. The skin on a bull's neck and shoulders is thick and tough to protect it during such battles. For the same reason, the neck of a bull walrus is covered with large bumps, a kind of warty armor, to shield itself from the jabs of another walrus's tusks. Even so, many male seals are injured during the battles of the breeding season, and some of them even die.

A male Hooker's sea lion smells the breath of a female. Her breath may identify her and tell him if she is ready to mate.

A male seal will fight to the death for one reason. If he does not, he may never win a mating partner, and so never be the father of a pup, or baby seal. The strongest fighters win the most female partners and father the most pups. A powerful male Hooker's sea lion may mate with two dozen females in one season. A tough-fighting male Antarctic fur seal may have 50 to 100 partners, and a large bull southern elephant seal may mate with over 200 females. A female seal, or cow, wants the largest and strongest male to be her partner. In this way, her pup will inherit the good qualities of its father and have the best chance to survive.

The Weddell seal lives along the coast of Antarctica,
farther south than any other seal.

Among land-breeding seals, males are larger—sometimes much larger—than their female partners. For example, a fur seal bull is often four to five times heavier than the female. The size difference is greatest in the elephant seals. A bull southern elephant seal may be ten times heavier than the female. Males need to be larger than the females because they fight so much. The bigger a seal is, the more males he can beat in a fight, and the more females he can win.

Ice-breeding seals, including harp seals, crabeaters, and Weddell seals, have an easier time mating. Most of the time, an ice-breeding male guards a single female until she is ready to mate. The males fight much less than land-breeding males, and as a result, they suffer fewer injuries. Among most of the ice-breeding seals, males and females are roughly the same size.

Seals
FUNFACT:

The most abundant seal in the world is the crabeater seal. Scientists estimate that the total population of crabeaters may exceed 20 million seals, which is more than all the other species of seals combined.

In most seals, the breeding season occurs around the same time the pups are being born. Usually a mother seal mates again within a few days to a few weeks after giving birth to a pup. Her next pup will be born approximately one year later, often on the same beach, and at the same time of the year. All male seals abandon their female partners soon after they mate with them. The fathers never care for their pups, and in fact, they probably never know them.

Seals
FUNFACT:

All seals molt their old fur and replace it with a fresh new coat every year. Most of them molt gradually, except for the elephant seals. When elephant seals molt, they stay on land and shed large patches of skin and fur that peel off their bodies like old paint from a building wall.

A male southern elephant seal may weigh ten times more than a female.
During mating, the male holds the female with his flipper and bites her on the neck.

On very crowded beaches, a newborn Hooker's sea lion may become separated from its mother, so it is very important for the two of them to quickly learn to recognize each other by their smell.

All seals give birth to a single pup. As soon as a pup is born, the mother spins around and nuzzles and sniffs her whining newborn. Mother fur seals are noisy, and they whimper and call to their pup. In a crowded seal colony, hundreds of pups may be born on the same day, and it is very important for a mother and a pup to recognize each other. They memorize the smell of each other's breath and the sound of each other's voices. Then, if they get separated, they can find each other easily with a sniff and a cry. Hungry pups will sometimes try to steal milk from a mother that is not their own. If they get sniffed and discovered, the angry mother may bite them and push them away.

Mother seals nurse and care for their pups in one of two ways: quickly or slowly. The earless seals, such as the hooded seal, the ringed seal, and the harbor seal are fast feeders. They nurse their pups with very rich, fatty milk. The milk is much thicker and has more fat than the thickest milkshake. The pups grow very quickly on such a fatty diet, and often double or triple their birth weight in less than two weeks. Then, when the pup looks like an overstuffed little sausage, the mother suddenly stops nursing and abandons it. Usually, the pup is only three or four weeks old. The shortest nursing period among all seals is seen in the hooded seal of the Arctic. The hooded seal pup nurses for just four days. In that short time, the silvery-blue pup balloons and doubles its birth weight, going from 44 pounds (20 kilograms) to 88 pounds (40 kilograms). It gains an amazing 11 pounds (5 kilograms) of fat every day. For humans to gain that much weight, they would have to gobble down 82 hamburgers and 23 large orders of french fries—every day for four days!

A nursing harp seal pup may suckle six or seven times a day.

Most earless seals are born on the surface of the sea ice in early spring. This cold, windy nursery is a dangerous place. Out in the open like this, the pups can easily be seen by predators such as arctic foxes and polar bears. To protect their pups, many mother seals give birth in areas of sea ice that frequently crack and break into pieces. Polar bears and foxes often stay away from this kind of ice because they don't want to fall into the cold water.

Because the ice may break at any moment, the seal pups face yet another danger. The newborn seals may be tossed into the icy water before they are big enough to swim and crawl out again. Because of this, an earless seal pup needs to grow very quickly and add a thick layer of blubber to keep its body warm if it should accidentally fall into the water.

Seals
FUNFACT:

The most playful of seals are young sea lions and fur seals. They chase each other, wrestle, and body surf. When there are no playmates, the young seals chew and play with pieces of driftwood, pebbles, or dried kelp—tossing the toys around and retrieving them.

This thin, young harp seal pup is waiting for its mother to return and nurse it. The adult seal in the water is ignoring the pup because it is probably not its mother.

A mother California sea lion will nurse her pup for one to three days, then leave it alone on the beach while she goes fishing for three to four days.

Fur seals and sea lions raise their families on land and do it differently than the ice-breeding seals. These seals raise their young slowly. Mother sea lions and fur seals produce milk that is less nourishing milk and contains less fat. As a result, their pups grow more slowly than the ice seals do, and the mothers must nurse them for many months. For example, a mother South American sea lion may nurse her pup for almost a year, and a mother Galapagos fur seal may nurse for two to three years.

Walrus mothers give birth on the ice in the same way as most of the earless seals, but the mothers raise their single pup like the fur seals and sea lions do. They stay with their pups for two years and nurse them throughout that time.

A bull walrus has few enemies, although scientists have seen them attacked and killed by large adult polar bears and killer whales.

Walruses feed by rooting along the ocean bottom, feeling for invertebrates (in-VER-tuh-brates), or small animals without backbones, with their sensitive whiskers. It takes a lot of practice for a young walrus to learn how to do this, so it needs to stay with its mother and nurse for several years before it can survive on its own.

The first few months of life are the most dangerous time for a pup. There is always the risk that it will become separated from its mother and starve to death. It may freeze to death in a frigid ice storm or drown when large waves wash over the beach. It can also be trampled to death by careless bulls fighting nearby. Once the pup reaches the age of one, it has a good chance to grow up to be an adult.

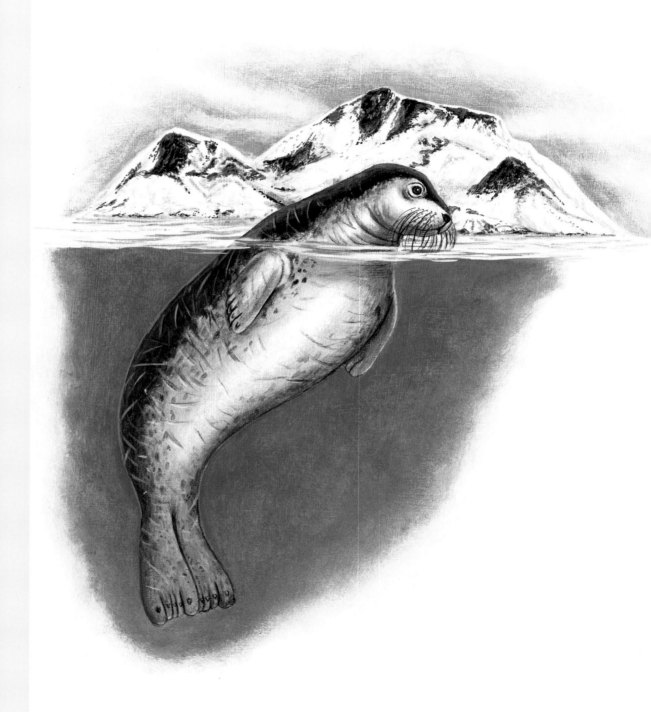

Adult life carries its own risks, and many predators have a taste for seal meat. In southern Africa, brown hyenas prey on sea lions that carelessly loaf along the beach at night. In South America, mountain lions hunt the rocky shorelines for unwary South American sea lions, and in British Columbia, coyotes stalk harbor seals along the coast. Some seals even eat their relatives. In the Arctic, bull walruses sometimes hunt and eat ringed seals, and in the Bering Sea of Alaska, hungry Steller sea lions kill young northern fur seals. In Antarctica, the leopard seal hunts fur seals, Weddell seals, Ross seals, and crabeaters. In fact, many adult crabeater seals have large scars on their sides or back from failed attacks by leopard seals.

Seals
FUNFACT:

Fur seals and sea lions are noisiest above the water, where they whimper, whine, bark, and roar. The earless seals, on the other hand, are usually quiet above the water but noisy underwater, where they warble, moan, buzz, chirp, and whistle.

This adult male Antarctic fur seal will not find a mate until it is at least seven years old. Until then, it stays on the edges of the colony and pretends to be tougher and bigger than it really is.

The biggest threat to all adult seals comes from in the ocean or beneath the ocean's surface. Wherever there are seal colonies, there are killer whales or great white sharks patrolling the waters offshore. No seal is too fast, too strong, or too large to be spared an attack by one of these fast-swimming hunters.

Both predators strike from below, rising out of the ocean blackness with speed and deadly force. Even shallow water doesn't keep them away. Great white sharks will attack elephant seals in waist-deep water, and killer whales in Argentina will throw themselves onto the beach to grab a sea lion resting by the water's edge.

Despite all the predators, the struggles to find food, and the battles of the breeding season, most seals survive to live for many years. Many seals live for 10 years or more, and some survive to the age of 25. The biggest threat to the survival of all seals comes from humans and the way they treat the oceans. When people pollute and overfish the oceans, it becomes more difficult for seals to survive. But it is never too late to make a change. Today, many people recognize that the health of the oceans is as important to the survival of humans as it is to the survival of seals. In the end, what is good for seals is also good for humans.

My POLAR ANIMALS Adventures

The date of my adventure: _____

The people who came with me: _____

_____

Where I went: _____

What polar animals I saw:

_____   _____

_____   _____

_____   _____

_____   _____

The date of my adventure: _____

The people who came with me: _____

_____

Where I went: _____

What polar animals I saw:

_____   _____

_____   _____

_____   _____

_____   _____

My POLAR ANIMALS Adventures

The date of my adventure: _____

The people who came with me: _____

_____

Where I went: _____

What polar animals I saw:

_____   _____

_____   _____

_____   _____

_____   _____

The date of my adventure: _____

The people who came with me: _____

_____

Where I went: _____

What polar animals I saw:

_____   _____

_____   _____

_____   _____

_____   _____

CARIBOU Index

PENGUINS Index

POLAR BEARS Index

SEALS Index

Internet Sites

You can find out more interesting information about Caribou, Penguins, Polar Bears, and Seals by visiting these web sites.

http://endangered.fws.gov/kids/index.html	U.S. Fish and Wildlife Service
www.animal.discovery.com	Discovery Channel Online
www.antarctic.com.au	Antarctic Adventure
www.aqwa.com	The Aquarium of Western Australia
www.bearbiology.com	International Association for Bear Research and Management
www.bear.org/Polar/PB_Home.html	North American Bear Center
www.EnchantedLearning.com	Disney Online
www.kidsgowild.com	Wildlife Conservation Society
www.kidsplanet.org	Defenders of Wildlife
www.learner.org/jnorth	Journey North
www.nationalgeographic.com/kids	National Geographic Society
www.nwf.org/kids	National Wildlife Federation
www.ocean.com/library/creaturefeature/Ocean.com	
www.pbs.org/edens/patagonia	PBS (Public Broadcast System)
www.penguin.net.nz	Penguins in New Zealand
www.pinnipeds.fsnet.co.uk	Seal Conservation Society
www.polarbearsalive.org	Polar Bears Alive
www.seabirds.org/penguins	International Penguin Conservation Work Group
www.seaworld.org/Pinnipeds/introduction.html	Sea World Page
www.tnc.org	The Nature Conservancy
www.wcs.org	Wildlife Conservation Society
www.worldwildlife.org/fun/kids.cfm	World Wildlife Fund
www.wwfcanada.org/satellite/wwfkids	Canadian World Wildlife Fund